7 REASONS WHY WE SHOULDN'T GET MARRIED

The unspoken consequences of saying "I DO"

I0490936

Ben Tories

Table of Contents

INTRODUCTION

Marriage is often seen as one of the most significant milestones in life, a rite of passage that marks the transition from singlehood to a committed partnership. It's an institution that has been revered across cultures and throughout history, with the idea of finding "the one" being romanticized in literature, movies, and pop culture.

However, the reality is that not all marriages are happy and fulfilling, and not all couples are truly meant to be together. In fact, the divorce rates in many countries are alarmingly high, indicating that a large percentage of marriages end in separation or divorce.

So why do so many people end up marrying the wrong person? What are the factors that lead to the breakdown of a marriage, and what can we do to avoid making this mistake ourselves?

This book explores these questions in depth, drawing on research, expert opinions, and personal anecdotes to provide a comprehensive analysis of why marrying the wrong person can have disastrous consequences.

The book will cover a range of topics, from the psychological and emotional factors that influence our partner's choices to the societal pressures that can lead us to make hasty or ill-considered decisions.

Marriage is a significant commitment that requires careful consideration and thoughtful decision-making. Choosing to marry the wrong person can have serious and long-lasting consequences that can impact every aspect of your life, from your emotional well-being to your financial stability.

While it may be tempting to rush into a marriage out of pressure from family or societal norms, it is crucial to take the time to ensure that you are making the right choice.

In this context, it is important to understand the reasons why you shouldn't get married to the wrong person, and why making the right call is critical for your overall happiness and success in life.

This essay will explore some of the most compelling reasons why it is essential to choose your partner wisely and how making the right decision can lead to a fulfilling and rewarding life together.

Marriage is a significant commitment that requires serious consideration and thought. It's a decision that will have a profound impact on your life, and it's essential to ensure that you are making the right choice for yourself.

While marriage can be a source of great joy and fulfillment, it can also bring challenges and difficulties that require determination and perseverance to overcome.

In today's society, there is a lot of pressure to conform to certain expectations when it comes to marriage. Family and friends may have their own ideas about what makes a successful marriage, and there may be societal norms and traditions that can make it challenging to stand your ground and make decisions that are in your best interest.

However, it's crucial to remember that your marriage is ultimately your own. You are the one who will be living with your partner, and it's important to prioritize your own happiness and well-being above all else.

This means standing your ground and making decisions that align with your values, beliefs, and goals, even if it goes against what others may think or expect.

By the end of this book, readers will have a clear understanding of the risks and pitfalls of marrying the wrong person and will be equipped with practical strategies for making more informed, thoughtful choices about their future partners.

Ultimately, "Why We Shouldn't Get Married" is a call to action for anyone who values their happiness and well-being, and wants to avoid the heartbreak and pain that can come from a failed marriage.

CHAPTER 1

Knowing Yourself

Before getting married, it's important to know yourself fully well. Marriage is a lifelong commitment, and it requires a deep understanding of oneself in order to build a healthy and successful relationship with another person.

Knowing yourself fully well means being aware of your strengths, weaknesses, values, and goals in life. It means having a clear understanding of what makes you happy, what motivates you, and what challenges you.

When you know yourself well, you are better equipped to communicate your needs and desires to your partner. You are more likely to be able to identify potential problems and work through them together. You are also more likely to make wise decisions that align with your values and goals, both individually and as a couple.

Without this level of self-awareness, you may enter into a marriage with unrealistic expectations or an incomplete understanding of your own needs and desires. This can lead to frustration, disappointment, and ultimately, the breakdown of the relationship.

To know yourself fully well, take the time to reflect on your past experiences, your personality, and your goals for the future. Consider seeking the help of a therapist or counselor to gain deeper insight into your own thought processes and emotional patterns.

By doing the work to know yourself fully well, you'll be able to enter into marriage with confidence, clarity, and a greater chance of success.

If you do not fully know yourself before getting married, you may end up making a decision that is not in your best interest. You may find yourself in a marriage that is not fulfilling, and you may feel lost and unsure of what you want out of life.

This can lead to feelings of regret, disappointment, and even resentment toward your partner.

Knowing yourself well before getting married is essential because it helps you understand what you want and need in a relationship. It allows you to set clear boundaries and communicate your expectations with your partner.

This helps you build a strong foundation for your marriage and ensures that you are both on the same page.

Additionally, knowing yourself well before getting married helps you make informed decisions about the future. It enables you to make choices that align with your values, goals, and priorities.

You can make choices that will help you grow and develop as a person, rather than holding you back.

In conclusion, getting married is a big decision, and it requires a deep understanding of yourself before you say "I do." Knowing yourself well enables you to make informed decisions about your future and ensures that you are making the right choice for yourself and your partner. Taking the time to know yourself before getting married can help you build a strong and fulfilling relationship that lasts a lifetime.

CHAPTER 2

What to Look for in a Partner

Choosing a partner is one of the most important decisions a person can make in their life. The right partner can bring joy, love, and support into your life, while the wrong one can bring stress, frustration, and heartache.

When selecting a partner, consider the following factors:

Compatibility: It's important to find someone who shares your values, interests, and goals. You should feel comfortable communicating with them and enjoy spending time with them. If you're not compatible, you'll likely struggle with communication and have a difficult time enjoying each other's company.

Respect: A good partner should respect your boundaries, opinions, and feelings. They should also be respectful of your family, friends, and other important relationships in your life. If your partner doesn't respect you or those close to you, it's a sign that they don't value you as a person.

Trustworthiness: A trustworthy partner is honest, reliable, and transparent. They should be truthful about their intentions, actions, and feelings. If your partner is constantly lying, hiding things from you, or breaking promises, it's a sign that they can't be trusted.

Communication: A healthy relationship is built on open and honest communication. You should be able to express your feelings and needs without fear of judgment or retaliation. If your partner is dismissive, defensive, or uninterested in what you have to say, it's a sign that they're not willing to put in the effort to make the relationship work.

Support: A good partner should be your biggest cheerleader. They should be supportive of your goals and dreams and encourage you to pursue them. If your partner is unsupportive or discouraging, it can lead to feelings of resentment and frustration.

It's important to note that if these criteria are not met, it's better to not enter into a relationship or to end an existing one. A relationship that lacks compatibility, respect, trustworthiness, communication, and support can lead to feelings of unhappiness, frustration, and even emotional or physical abuse.

It's better to wait for a partner who meets these criteria than to settle for someone who doesn't, as it will ultimately lead to a healthier and more fulfilling relationship.

The role of personality traits in compatibility

Personality traits can play a crucial role in determining compatibility between individuals. Compatibility refers to the ability of two individuals to coexist and work together in harmony without conflicts. It encompasses various aspects such as emotional compatibility, intellectual compatibility, physical compatibility, and spiritual compatibility.

When it comes to personality traits, each individual has their own unique set of characteristics that shape their behavior, emotions, and attitudes. These traits can influence how well they get along with others and whether they are compatible with them or not.

For example, individuals who have similar personality traits are more likely to be compatible with each other. People who share common interests, values, and beliefs tend to have a better understanding of each other, which can lead to a deeper connection.

On the other hand, individuals with opposing personality traits may find it difficult to get along with each other. For instance, if one person is highly extroverted and outgoing while the other is introverted and reserved, it can create conflicts in their relationship.

Some of the personality traits that can impact compatibility include:

Openness: Individuals who are open-minded, creative, and curious tend to be more compatible with others who share these traits.

Conscientiousness: People who are responsible, organized, and dependable often work well with others who also value these traits.

Agreeableness: Individuals who are kind, empathetic, and cooperative tend to be more compatible with those who share similar values.

Neuroticism: People who are prone to anxiety, stress, and negative emotions may struggle to form strong relationships with individuals who have a more positive outlook.

Extraversion: Individuals who are outgoing, talkative, and energetic tend to be more compatible with others who share these traits.

In summary, personality traits can play a significant role in determining compatibility between individuals. While having similar personality traits can create a stronger connection, it's important to remember that differences can also bring diversity and richness to a relationship. Ultimately, communication, mutual respect, and a willingness to compromise are key to maintaining a successful and compatible relationship.

Common personality clashes in romantic relationships

There are many reasons why people choose to get married, but it's important to remember that not everyone is cut out for marriage, especially if there are common personality clashes present in the relationship.

One of the most common reasons why couples experience personality clashes is differences in communication styles. Some people prefer to communicate openly and directly, while others prefer to keep their feelings and thoughts to themselves. This can lead to misunderstandings, frustration, and even resentment.

Another common personality clash is conflict resolution. Some people prefer to confront conflict head-on, while others avoid it at all costs. This can lead to unaddressed issues, pent-up anger, and resentment.

Other common personality clashes include differences in values and goals, differences in lifestyle preferences, and differences in expectations for the relationship. When these clashes go unresolved, they can lead to significant challenges in the relationship and even contribute to its ultimate demise.

It's important to note that these clashes are not always a sign of a doomed relationship. However, they do require attention and effort to overcome.

It's important to recognize and acknowledge these differences and work together to find a way to communicate, resolve conflicts, and work towards shared goals.

If these personality clashes persist and become too difficult to manage, it may be a sign that marriage is not the best choice for the couple. It's important to prioritize your own well-being and happiness, even if that means making the difficult decision to end a relationship.

In the end, it's up to each individual to determine whether marriage is the right choice for them, taking into account the potential personality clashes that may arise. It's important to approach marriage with open eyes and an understanding that it requires ongoing effort and communication to make it work.

CHAPTER 3

Red Flags in a Relationship

Red flags in a relationship are warning signs that something may be amiss. They can be behaviors, actions, or attitudes that make you feel uncomfortable or uneasy, and may indicate that the relationship is not healthy or sustainable. They are often subtle and can be ignored, but if they become too frequent or intense, they can be a sign of something more serious. It's important to pay attention to these red flags, as they can be an indication that you should not get married.

Some common red flags in a relationship include:

Controlling behavior - if your partner is controlling, manipulative, or tries to limit your independence or autonomy, it can be a sign that they don't respect your boundaries.

Lack of trust - if your partner is constantly questioning your loyalty or accusing you of cheating, it can be a sign that they don't trust you, which can lead to insecurity and jealousy.

Disrespectful behavior - if your partner belittles you, makes fun of you, or dismisses your opinions or feelings, it can be a sign that they don't value you as an equal partner.

Dishonesty - if your partner lies to you or keeps important information from you, it can be a sign that they don't value honesty and openness in the relationship.

Abuse - any kind of physical, emotional, or sexual abuse is a major red flag and should never be ignored.

These red flags can have a significant impact on your well-being and happiness. They can lead to feelings of anxiety, depression, and low self-esteem, as well as damage your ability to trust others in future relationships.

If you notice these red flags in a relationship, it's important to address them with your partner and attempt to work through them together. However, if the issues persist and cannot be resolved, it may be a sign that the relationship is not healthy or sustainable.

Getting married when you notice these red flags is not recommended, as it can lead to a lifetime of unhappiness and possibly even abuse. It's important to prioritize your own well-being and safety, even if it means ending the relationship or seeking outside help to address the issues. Remember, you deserve to be in a relationship where you feel respected, valued, and safe.

The pitfalls of falling in love too quickly

Falling in love can be a wonderful experience, but it can also be dangerous if you fall too quickly. When you fall in love too quickly, you may not have a chance to get to know the person well enough before you start feeling deeply attached to them. This can lead to a number of pitfalls that can be damaging to your emotional well-being and your relationships.

Here are some of the pitfalls of falling in love too quickly:

Idealizing the person: When you fall in love too quickly, you may put the person on a pedestal and idealize them. You may think that they are perfect and overlook their flaws. This can lead to disappointment later on when you realize that they are not the person you thought they were.

Ignoring red flags: When you fall in love too quickly, you may overlook red flags that would have been obvious if you had taken the time to get to know the person better. You may be so blinded by your feelings that you ignore warning signs that the person may not be a good match for you.

Moving too fast: When you fall in love too quickly, you may move too fast in the relationship. You may want to spend all your time with the person and rush into things like moving in together or getting married before you are ready. This can put a strain on the relationship and cause problems down the line.

Losing your identity: When you fall in love too quickly, you may become so focused on the other person that you lose sight of your own goals and interests. You may start to prioritize the relationship over everything else in your life, which can be unhealthy and lead to codependency.

Feeling intense emotions: When you fall in love too quickly, you may experience intense emotions that can be overwhelming. You may feel like you can't live without the person and become overly dependent on them for your happiness. This can be dangerous if the relationship ends, as it can lead to depression and other emotional issues.

Overall, falling in love too quickly can be risky. It's important to take your time getting to know someone before you become emotionally invested in the relationship. This can help you avoid the pitfalls of idealizing the person, ignoring red flags, moving too fast, losing your identity, and feeling intense emotions.

The dangers of ignoring red flags or warning signs early on

Ignoring red flags or warning signs early on in a relationship can lead to serious consequences down the road. While it's natural to be excited about a new relationship, it's important to be aware of potential warning signs that may indicate that the relationship could be unhealthy or dangerous.

Some common red flags to look out for include:

Disrespectful behavior: If your partner shows disrespect towards you, your boundaries, or other people, it can be a major red flag. Disrespect can take many forms, such as belittling or dismissing your opinions, talking down to you, or making fun of you in public.

Control issues: If your partner tries to control your behavior, whom you see, or what you do, it's a sign of an unhealthy dynamic. This can include monitoring your phone or social media, limiting your access to friends and family, or making decisions for you without your input.

Dishonesty: Honesty is the foundation of any healthy relationship. If your partner lies to you or withholds important information, it can erode trust and lead to bigger issues down the line.

Blaming and criticism: If your partner is quick to blame you for everything that goes wrong, or frequently criticizes you in a way that makes you feel bad about yourself, it's a major red flag. Healthy relationships are built on mutual respect and support, not criticism and blame.

Intensity and obsession: While it's natural to feel passionate about a new relationship if your partner is overly intense or obsessive, it can be a warning sign. This can include constantly texting or calling you, demanding all of your time and attention, or making grandiose declarations of love and commitment very early on.

Ignoring these red flags or warning signs can have serious consequences. If you overlook disrespectful or controlling behavior, it can escalate over time, leading to emotional or physical abuse. If you continue to tolerate dishonesty, blame, or criticism, it can erode your self-esteem and lead to feelings of resentment or depression. And if you stay with a partner who is overly intense or obsessive, it can lead to feelings of suffocation or being trapped in the relationship.

In short, it's important to pay attention to red flags early on in a relationship and address them proactively. If you see warning signs that your partner may be abusive or controlling, it's important to seek help from a trusted friend or professional. Remember that you deserve to be in a healthy and respectful relationship, and it's never too late to make changes that prioritize your well-being.

CHAPTER 4

Dealing with a Wrong Choice

Making a wrong choice in a relationship or marriage can be a difficult situation to handle. It can leave you feeling overwhelmed with regret, frustration, and disappointment. However, it's important to remember that every mistake is an opportunity to learn and grow.

Here are some steps to help you deal with a wrong choice in a relationship or marriage:

Acknowledge your feelings: It's important to acknowledge and accept your feelings of disappointment, anger, sadness, or any other emotion that you may be experiencing. Don't suppress your emotions, as this will only make it harder to move forward. allow yourself to feel your emotions fully, instead.

Take responsibility: Take responsibility for your choices and actions. Don't blame others for your mistakes. Accept that you made the wrong choice and take ownership of it.

Assess the situation: Take some time to assess the situation objectively. Look at the reasons why you made the wrong choice and consider what you could have done differently. This will help you learn from your mistake and avoid making the same mistake again in the future.

Communicate with your partner: If you're in a relationship or marriage, it's important to communicate openly and honestly with your partner about your feelings. Let them know what happened and how you're feeling. Be willing to listen to their perspective and work together to find a way forward.

Seek support: Don't be afraid to seek support from friends, family, or a therapist. Talking to someone about your feelings and getting their perspective can be helpful in dealing with a wrong choice.

Focus on the present: Don't dwell on the past or beat yourself up for making the wrong choice. Focus on the present and what you can do now to move forward. Learn from your mistake, but don't let it define you.

Take action: Take action to make things right. If you're in a relationship or marriage, work with your partner to find a way forward. If the relationship is irreparable, take steps to move on and start anew.

Dealing with a wrong choice in a relationship or marriage can be a challenging and emotional experience. However, by acknowledging your feelings, taking responsibility, assessing the situation, communicating with your partner, seeking support, focusing on the present, and taking action, you can learn from your mistake and move forward in a positive way.

The risks of staying in a relationship out of fear or complacency

Staying in a relationship out of fear or complacency can be incredibly risky and detrimental to one's well-being. While it may seem comfortable to remain in a relationship that is familiar and predictable, it can also prevent personal growth and happiness.

One of the primary risks of staying in a relationship out of fear is that it can lead to a lack of self-esteem and confidence. If you are afraid of being alone or fear that you cannot find anyone else who will love you, you may start to believe that you are not worthy of love or affection. This can lead to a cycle of low self-esteem and self-doubt, which can be difficult to break.

Another risk of staying in a relationship out of fear or complacency is that it can prevent personal growth and development. If you are in a relationship that is comfortable and predictable, you may not feel motivated to pursue your own interests or try new things. This can lead to a lack of personal fulfillment and a sense of stagnation in life.

Furthermore, staying in a relationship out of fear or complacency can lead to resentment and dissatisfaction over time. If you are not happy in your relationship but are too afraid to leave, you may start to harbor negative feelings towards your partner.

This can lead to a breakdown in communication and trust, and ultimately, the relationship may become toxic and unhealthy.

Finally, staying in a relationship out of fear or complacency can prevent you from finding true love and happiness.

If you are in a relationship that is not fulfilling, you may miss out on the opportunity to meet someone who is truly compatible with you and who can help you grow and develop as a person.

In conclusion, while it may seem safe and comfortable to stay in a relationship out of fear or complacency, it can be incredibly risky and detrimental to one's well-being.

If you are not happy in your relationship, it is important to have the courage to leave and pursue your own happiness and personal growth.

Signs that you may be settling for less than you deserve

Relationships are supposed to be a source of happiness, fulfillment, and growth. However, sometimes we may find ourselves settling for less than we deserve in a relationship.

This can happen for a variety of reasons, such as fear of being alone, pressure from family or society, or low self-esteem. Here are some signs that you may be settling for less than you deserve in a relationship:

You constantly make excuses for your partner's behavior: If you find yourself constantly justifying your partner's actions or making excuses for their behavior, it may be a sign that you are settling for less.

You should not have to justify someone else's actions or make excuses for them.

Your partner doesn't treat you with respect: Respect is a fundamental component of any healthy relationship. If your partner doesn't treat you with the respect you deserve, such as by belittling you, insulting you, or ignoring your feelings, you may be settling for less.

You're not happy: If you're not happy in your relationship, it's a clear sign that something is wrong. While all relationships have their ups and downs, if you're consistently unhappy, it may be a sign that you're settling for less than you deserve.

You feel like you're compromising too much: Compromise is important in any relationship, but if you feel like you're constantly giving up what you want or need to make your partner happy, it may be a sign that you're settling for less.

Your partner doesn't support your goals and dreams: A supportive partner should encourage you to pursue your goals and dreams, not hold you back. If your partner doesn't support your aspirations, it may be a sign that you're settling for less.

If you recognize any of these signs in your relationship, it's important to take a step back and evaluate whether you're truly happy and fulfilled. Going into a marriage with these signs can lead to a lifetime of unhappiness and regret.

It's better to address these issues before getting married and potentially making a mistake that could have long-lasting consequences.

Remember that you deserve to be with someone who treats you with respect, supports your goals, and makes you happy.

Don't settle for less than you deserve in a relationship or a marriage. It's better to be single and happy than to be in an unhappy relationship or marriage.

How to break free from a stagnant or unfulfilling relationship

Breaking free from a stagnant or unfulfilling relationship can be a difficult and painful process, but it is necessary for your own well-being and happiness.

Here are some steps that can help you break free from such a relationship:

Acknowledge your feelings: Before you can take any action, it is important to recognize and acknowledge your feelings.

Are you feeling unhappy, unfulfilled, or unappreciated in the relationship?

Take some time to reflect on your emotions and be honest with yourself.

Communicate your feelings: Once you have acknowledged your feelings, it is important to communicate them to your partner. Be clear and honest about how you feel and what you need from the relationship.

Give your partner a chance to respond and listen to what they have to say.

Take a break: If you need some time and space to think, take a break from the relationship. This could be a temporary separation or a break from communication.

Use this time to reflect on your feelings and what you want from the relationship.

Seek support: Breaking free from a relationship can be emotionally challenging, so it is important to seek support from friends, family, or a therapist.

Talking to someone who can offer a listening ear and unbiased advice can be helpful.

Set boundaries: If you have decided to end the relationship, it is important to set boundaries with your partner. Be clear about what you expect from the breakup and stick to your boundaries.

Take care of yourself: After a breakup, it is important to take care of yourself. This could involve self-care activities such as exercise, meditation, or spending time with loved ones.

Focus on your own well-being and give yourself time to heal.

Breaking free from a stagnant or unfulfilling relationship can be challenging, but it is important to prioritize your own well-being and happiness.

Remember that you deserve to be in a relationship that makes you feel loved, appreciated, and fulfilled.

CHAPTER 5

Misaligned Values and Goals

Misaligned values and goals refer to situations in which two people in a relationship have fundamentally different beliefs and desires about what they want in life and what is important to them.

This misalignment can lead to significant challenges in a relationship, particularly in a marriage, as it affects the couple's ability to make decisions together and pursue common objectives.

When partners have different values and goals, they may struggle to find common ground on important issues such as career aspirations, financial management, family planning, and lifestyle choices.

For instance, if one partner places a high value on career success and financial stability, while the other prioritizes work-life balance and pursuing creative interests, they may have difficulty reconciling these divergent goals and may find it challenging to make important decisions together.

These differences can lead to conflicts, misunderstandings, and a lack of trust, as partners may feel unsupported or even threatened by the other's priorities. For example, if one partner is focused on saving money for a future down payment on a house, while the other wants to spend more money on travel and experiences, they may find it difficult to agree on how to allocate their resources and may feel resentful of each other's preferences.

Overall, misaligned values and goals can be a significant source of tension in relationships and marriages. To address these challenges, partners need to engage in open communication, active listening, and compromise, to find ways to support each other's goals while also pursuing shared objectives.

Counseling or therapy can also be helpful in identifying and addressing these issues in a constructive and healthy manner.

The importance of shared values and goals in a successful partnership

Shared values and goals are essential components of any successful relationship, whether it is a romantic partnership, a friendship, or a business partnership. When two people have shared values and goals, they are more likely to work together harmoniously and achieve their desired outcomes.

In this article, we will explore why shared values and goals are important in a successful relationship.

Shared values create a sense of mutual understanding When two people share the same values, they can understand each other better. They are more likely to have similar beliefs about what is right and wrong, what is important, and what their priorities are.

This can help to create a sense of mutual understanding and respect, which is vital for any successful relationship.

Shared values provide a sense of direction

When two people share the same values, they can work together to achieve a common purpose. They know what they want to achieve, and they have a clear direction to follow. This can help to keep them motivated and focused, even when they encounter obstacles or challenges.

Shared goals create a sense of teamwork

When two people share the same goals, they can work together as a team. They can pool their resources, skills, and expertise to achieve their desired outcomes. This can help to create a sense of camaraderie and teamwork, which is essential for any successful relationship.

Shared goals provide a sense of accomplishment

When two people work together to achieve a common goal, they can experience a sense of accomplishment and satisfaction. They know that they have achieved something meaningful and valuable, and they can feel proud of their efforts. This can help to strengthen their relationship and build a sense of mutual respect and admiration.

In conclusion, shared values and goals are important components of any successful relationship. They create a sense of mutual understanding, provide a sense of direction, create a sense of teamwork, and provide a sense of accomplishment. When two people share the same values and goals, they are more likely to work together harmoniously and achieve their desired outcomes.

How to identify potential conflicts early on

Identifying potential conflicts early on in a relationship can help prevent misunderstandings and disagreements from escalating into larger problems.

Here are some tips for recognizing and addressing potential conflicts early on in a relationship:

Pay attention to communication patterns: Communication is key to any successful relationship, and paying attention to how you and your partner communicate with each other can help you identify potential conflicts early on. If you notice that your partner is often dismissive or ignores your concerns, this could be a red flag.

Be aware of differences in values: While it's important to have shared interests and values in a relationship, it's also natural for partners to have some differences. However, if these differences are significant and not addressed early on, they could lead to conflicts down the line. Take note of any values or beliefs that you and your partner disagree on and discuss them openly.

Keep an eye out for patterns of behavior: People's behavior patterns can reveal a lot about their personalities and how they approach relationships. If your partner has a pattern of controlling or manipulative behavior, this could be a potential conflict in the making.

Take note of how conflicts are handled: No relationship is perfect, and conflicts are bound to happen. However, it's important to pay attention to how conflicts are handled in your relationship. If your partner consistently avoids or refuses to address conflicts, this could be a sign of trouble.

Talk openly and honestly: Communication is the key to any healthy relationship, and open and honest communication is especially important when it comes to identifying potential conflicts. Don't be afraid to express your concerns to your partner and work together to find solutions that work for both of you.

By paying attention to communication patterns, differences in values, behavior patterns, and conflict management styles, and having open and honest conversations, you can identify potential conflicts early on in a relationship and work together to prevent them from becoming larger problems.

Remember, healthy relationships require effort and ongoing communication, so it's important to stay vigilant and proactive.

Strategies for communicating and negotiating differences

Every relationship has its fair share of differences and disagreements, which can be a source of stress and tension if not dealt with properly. Communication and negotiation are key skills for navigating differences in a relationship. Here are some strategies for effectively communicating and negotiating differences in a relationship:

Start with empathy: Before jumping into the discussion, take a moment to consider your partner's perspective. Try to see the situation from their point of view and acknowledge their feelings. Starting the conversation with empathy can help create a more positive and open atmosphere.

Use "I" statements: Instead of blaming or accusing your partner, use "I" statements to express how you feel. For example, say "I feel hurt when you don't listen to me" instead of "You never listen to me."

Listen actively: Active listening involves not only hearing what your partner is saying but also trying to understand their perspective. Ask questions to clarify their position and show that you are genuinely interested in what they have to say.

Avoid attacking or criticizing: Criticizing or attacking your partner can make them defensive and less likely to be receptive to your point of view. Focus on the issue at hand and avoid making sweeping generalizations about your partner's behavior or character.

Look for compromise: Negotiation involves finding a middle ground that both partners can agree on. Look for solutions that meet both of your needs and try to find a compromise that works for both of you.

Take a break if needed: If the conversation becomes too heated or overwhelming, take a break and come back to it later. It's okay to pause the conversation and take time to calm down before continuing.

Practice forgiveness: Remember that nobody is perfect, and mistakes will be made. Practice forgiveness and let go of past grievances to move forward in your relationship.

In conclusion, effective communication and negotiation skills are essential for resolving differences in a relationship. By starting with empathy, using "I" statements, listening actively, avoiding criticism, looking for compromise, taking breaks if needed, and practicing forgiveness, you can navigate differences in your relationship with greater success.

CHAPTER 6

Making a Better Choice

Making a better choice in a relationship is crucial for a fulfilling and lasting partnership. Many people rush into relationships without considering whether their partner is truly compatible with them, or if they are just settling for someone who is convenient or available at the time. However, it is important to take the time to choose wisely and find someone who is truly right for you.

When choosing a partner, it is important to look beyond superficial qualities and focus on values, interests, and compatibility. These are the things that will ultimately determine whether you are happy together in the long run.

Take the time to get to know your potential partner and ask important questions about their goals, values, and priorities.

This will help you determine whether you are on the same page and can build a future together.

One of the most important reasons not to marry the wrong person is that it can lead to a lifetime of unhappiness and unfulfillment. While it may be tempting to settle for someone who is available or convenient, it is important to remember that marriage is a serious commitment that should not be entered into lightly.

If you marry someone who is not truly compatible with you, you may find yourself feeling trapped, unfulfilled, and resentful.

Additionally, marrying the wrong person can have serious consequences for your mental and emotional health. Research shows that unhappy marriages can lead to a range of negative health outcomes, including depression, anxiety, and even physical health problems.

It is important to prioritize your own well-being and choose a partner who is supportive, loving, and compatible with you.

Ultimately, making a better choice in a relationship requires patience, self-awareness, and a willingness to be honest with yourself and your potential partner. Take the time to evaluate your own needs and desires, and be willing to walk away from a relationship that is not right for you. By making a thoughtful and intentional choice, you can build a happy and fulfilling partnership that lasts a lifetime.

The importance of emotional intelligence in choosing a partner

Emotional intelligence (EI) is the ability to understand and manage one's own emotions as well as the emotions of others requires abilities like motivation, self-control, self-awareness, and social skills. When it comes to choosing a romantic partner, emotional intelligence can play a crucial role in determining the success of the relationship.

Here are a few reasons why:

Communication: Any healthy relationship must have open lines of communication as its foundation. People with high emotional intelligence are generally better at expressing their feelings, listening actively to their partner, and resolving conflicts peacefully. They are more likely to use "I" statements instead of blaming their partner, and they can express their needs and wants in a non-confrontational manner.

Empathy: Empathy is the ability to put yourself in someone else's shoes and understand how they are feeling. This is an essential component of emotional intelligence. People with high EI can empathize with their partner's emotions and respond in a supportive and caring way. This creates a sense of intimacy and connection that can strengthen the bond between partners.

Understanding emotions: Emotional intelligence allows individuals to identify, understand, and regulate their own emotions as well as those of their partner. This means they are less likely to react impulsively or say hurtful things when they are upset. Instead, they can take a step back and process their emotions in a healthy way before responding. This helps to create a safe and stable emotional environment in the relationship.

Conflict resolution: No relationship is without conflict, but people with high EI are better equipped to navigate disagreements and find solutions that work for both partners. They can separate their emotions from the problem at hand and focus on finding a resolution that meets both partners' needs.

In summary, emotional intelligence is an important factor to consider when choosing a partner. People with high EI are better communicators, more empathetic, better at understanding emotions, and better at resolving conflicts. These skills can contribute to a healthy, fulfilling relationship that can stand the test of time.

Looking for shared interests and commonalities beyond physical attraction

When it comes to forming a meaningful and fulfilling relationship, physical attraction can be an important factor, but it's not the only one that matters. Looking for shared interests and commonalities beyond physical attraction can be an essential aspect of building a lasting and meaningful relationship.

The first step in discovering shared interests is to spend time getting to know the other person. Spend time talking and asking questions about their hobbies, passions, and interests.

Listen carefully and be open-minded to learn more about them. It's essential to find out what motivates and excites them, what they enjoy doing in their free time, and what goals they have for themselves.

Once you have a better understanding of their interests and passions, it's essential to evaluate whether you share any of these same interests. For example, if they enjoy hiking, you may want to suggest going on a hike together.

If they love to cook, you could plan a cooking date. By participating in activities that both of you enjoy, you can strengthen your connection and create lasting memories together.

In addition to shared interests, it's also important to look for commonalities beyond hobbies and activities. These may include shared values, beliefs, and goals for the future.

For example, if you both value honesty and integrity, you may find it easier to communicate effectively and build trust in your relationship.

Finding commonalities beyond physical attraction can also help you to build a deeper emotional connection with your partner.

By sharing your thoughts, feelings, and experiences, you can develop a better understanding of each other's perspectives and create a more meaningful bond.

In conclusion, while physical attraction can be important in a relationship, it's not the only thing that matters. By looking for shared interests and commonalities beyond physical attraction, you can build a deeper connection with your partner and create a more fulfilling and lasting relationship.

The role of family and community in choosing a life partner

The decision to choose a life partner is one of the most significant and life-altering decisions a person can make. While it is ultimately an individual's choice, family and community can play a significant role in the decision-making process.

In many cultures, the involvement of family and community in choosing a life partner is considered essential, and their input is highly valued.

One of the most significant benefits of involving family and community in selecting a life partner is the assurance of compatibility. In some cultures, families have arranged marriages for centuries, ensuring that the individuals they choose are well-suited for each other in terms of religion, socioeconomic status, and cultural values. T

his can be especially important in societies where the family unit is highly valued, and divorce is stigmatized.

Moreover, families and communities can provide a network of support and guidance throughout the selection process. They can offer valuable advice on what to look for in a partner, share their experiences and insights, and help identify potential partners who may be a good match.

This can be especially important for individuals who are unsure of what they are looking for in a partner or may have limited experience in dating or relationships.

In addition, involving family and community in choosing a life partner can strengthen social connections and promote social harmony. By involving parents, grandparents, and other members of the family, the decision becomes a family affair, promoting unity and shared responsibility.

This can help ensure that the relationship is supported and accepted by the broader community, reducing the chances of social isolation or conflict.

However, it is also important to recognize that the role of family and community in choosing a life partner varies across cultures and individuals. Some people may value their independence and prefer to make the decision themselves, while others may come from a culture where the family's role is paramount.

Ultimately, the decision to involve family and community in selecting a life partner is a personal one that should be based on individual circumstances and preferences.

In conclusion, the role of family and community in choosing a life partner is significant and can provide many benefits, including increased compatibility, social support, and community harmony.

However, it is important to balance these benefits with individual preferences and cultural norms to ensure a successful and fulfilling relationship.

Balancing individual needs with the needs of a partnership, including compromise and mutual support

Maintaining a healthy and successful partnership requires balancing individual needs with the needs of the relationship itself. It is important to recognize that every individual in a partnership has unique needs, desires, and goals, and being able to find a balance between them is crucial for long-term happiness and satisfaction.

In any relationship, compromise is key. It is not uncommon for partners to have different priorities or preferences, but the ability to find common ground and make mutual concessions is essential.

Both parties should be willing to give a little to ensure the success of the partnership.

Additionally, mutual support is a fundamental aspect of a healthy partnership. This means being there for each other through good times and bad, providing emotional and practical support, and working together towards shared goals.

It is important to acknowledge that individual success and happiness are directly linked to the success and happiness of the partnership.

Communication is also critical in balancing individual needs with those of the relationship. Partners should be open and honest with each other about their needs and expectations.

This can help to avoid misunderstandings and resentment and allow for constructive dialogue and problem-solving.

In summary, balancing individual needs with the needs of a partnership requires compromise, mutual support, and effective communication.

By prioritizing the success of the relationship and working together towards shared goals, partners can create a fulfilling and sustainable partnership that allows each individual to thrive.

CHAPTER 7

Moving Forward

Moving forward in a relationship is an important and exciting step that requires a lot of care and consideration. Whether it's moving forward in a romantic relationship or a platonic one, the decision to take things to the next level should be made after careful thought and communication.

One of the most important things to consider when moving forward in a relationship is whether both parties are on the same page. It's essential to have open and honest communication about what each person wants and expects from the relationship.

This includes discussing topics like commitment, boundaries, and future goals. If both parties are not on the same page, it's important to work through any issues before moving forward.

Another important factor to consider is timing. Moving forward in a relationship requires a significant amount of emotional investment, and it's essential to ensure that both parties are ready for that commitment. Rushing into things can cause unnecessary stress and strain on the relationship, so it's crucial to take things at a pace that feels comfortable for everyone involved.

In addition to communication and timing, it's essential to approach moving forward in a relationship with an open mind and heart. This means being willing to compromise, being understanding of each other's needs and feelings, and being supportive of each other's growth and development.

Finally, it's important to remember that moving forward in a relationship is not a one-time decision. It's an ongoing process that requires continuous effort and communication. It's important to regularly check in with each other and make sure that everyone is still on the same page and that the relationship is still meeting everyone's needs.

In conclusion, moving forward in a relationship is an exciting and significant step that requires a lot of care and consideration. With open communication, a willingness to compromise, and a commitment to ongoing effort and growth, it's possible to create a healthy and fulfilling relationship that can stand the test of time.

Strategies for avoiding common pitfalls and choosing the right partner

When it comes to choosing a partner, there are many potential pitfalls that one can fall into. These can include rushing into a relationship too quickly, ignoring red flags, and overlooking important compatibility factors. However, there are several strategies that can help you avoid these common pitfalls and choose the right partner for you.

Take your time: It can be tempting to jump into a relationship quickly, especially if you feel a strong connection with someone. However, it's important to take your time and get to know the person before committing to a relationship. This will give you the opportunity to assess their values, personality, and compatibility with you.

Pay attention to red flags: Red flags are warning signs that indicate potential problems in a relationship. These can include things like a lack of communication, dishonesty, or a history of unhealthy relationships. It's important to pay attention to these red flags and address them before they become bigger issues.

Consider compatibility: Compatibility is a key factor in any successful relationship. It's important to consider factors like shared interests, values, and goals when choosing a partner. This will help ensure that you're on the same page and have a strong foundation for your relationship.

Look for emotional intelligence: Emotional intelligence is the ability to recognize and manage your own emotions, as well as understand and empathize with the emotions of others. It's an important trait in any partner, as it helps promote healthy communication and understanding in a relationship.

Communicate openly and honestly: Open and honest communication is essential in any relationship. It's important to be upfront about your needs, wants, and expectations from the beginning. This will help ensure that you and your partner are on the same page and can work together to build a strong and healthy relationship.

Trust your instincts: Finally, it's important to trust your instincts when choosing a partner. If something doesn't feel right or you have a bad feeling about a potential partner, it's important to listen to that intuition and proceed with caution.

In summary, choosing the right partner requires taking your time, paying attention to red flags, considering compatibility, looking for emotional intelligence, communicating openly and honestly, and trusting your instincts. By following these strategies, you can avoid common pitfalls and build a strong and healthy relationship with the right partner.

The importance of ongoing communication and self-reflection in a healthy relationship

Ongoing communication and self-reflection are both essential ingredients for a healthy relationship. They help build and maintain trust, understanding, and intimacy between partners.

Effective communication involves not just talking, but also actively listening and responding to your partner's needs and concerns. This means making an effort to understand your partner's perspective and feelings, and being open and honest about your own. It's important to communicate regularly, not just when there is a problem or conflict. Regular communication helps build intimacy and keeps both partners connected.

Self-reflection is also crucial for a healthy relationship. It involves taking a step back and reflecting on your own thoughts, feelings, and behaviors, and how they impact your relationship. Self-reflection helps you to better understand yourself and your partner, identify patterns of behavior that may be causing issues in the relationship, and make positive changes.

Self-reflection also helps you to be more accountable for your actions and to take responsibility for any mistakes you may have made. By recognizing your own flaws and working on them, you can become a better partner and build a stronger relationship.

In a healthy relationship, ongoing communication and self-reflection work together to create a safe and supportive environment where both partners feel heard, understood, and valued. By making an effort to communicate regularly and reflect on your own behavior, you can build a stronger, more fulfilling relationship with your partner.

Embracing the process of finding a compatible partner and building a fulfilling life together

Embracing the process of finding a compatible partner and building a fulfilling life together is an essential aspect of a healthy and happy relationship. It requires patience, commitment, and a willingness to grow together.

The journey toward finding a compatible partner can be challenging, but it is important to approach it with an open mind and heart. Instead of focusing solely on physical attraction or superficial qualities, it is essential to prioritize values, personality traits, and shared interests.

These factors are crucial in building a strong foundation for a long-lasting relationship.

Once you have found a compatible partner, it is essential to approach building a fulfilling life together as a collaborative effort. Communication, trust, and respect are key elements in building a healthy relationship.

It is important to be open and honest about your expectations, desires, and goals for the future. This will help ensure that both partners are on the same page and working towards a common goal.

Building a fulfilling life together also requires a willingness to compromise and adapt to change. As individuals, we all have our own unique perspectives and ways of doing things.

However, when building a life together, it is important to be flexible and willing to compromise in order to find solutions that work for both partners.

Finally, it is important to remember that building a fulfilling life together is an ongoing process. It requires continued effort, patience, and a willingness to learn and grow together.

By embracing the process and committing to building a strong foundation, you can create a relationship that is fulfilling, loving, and enduring.

CONCLUSION

Choosing the wrong partner can have a significant impact on your life, causing emotional pain, mental distress, and even physical harm. It can leave you feeling drained, hopeless, and stuck in a toxic relationship that drains your energy and confidence.

A bad partner can damage your self-esteem, cause you to doubt yourself, and make you feel like you are not good enough. Moreover, it can prevent you from growing and reaching your full potential.

When you are in a relationship with someone who is not compatible with you, you may struggle with communication, trust, and understanding. You may also feel isolated and lonely, as your needs are not being met. In some cases, you may even experience abuse, whether emotional or physical.

Choosing the wrong partner can impact not only your emotional well-being but also your future. It can prevent you from achieving your goals, pursuing your passions, and living a fulfilling life. It can hold you back and make it difficult for you to move forward.

In conclusion, choosing the wrong partner can have a detrimental impact on your life. It is important to take the time to reflect on what you want and need in a relationship and choose a partner who is compatible with you. A healthy relationship should uplift you, support you, and encourage you to grow.

In conclusion, getting married is a significant life decision that should not be taken lightly. It is important to carefully consider your feelings and intentions towards your partner before making such a commitment. Marriage involves a lot of emotional, financial, and legal responsibilities that can have a significant impact on your life.

If you are not sure about your partner or the relationship, it is best to wait and continue to explore your options. Rushing into a marriage with doubts and uncertainty may lead to unhappiness and regret in the future. Therefore, it is crucial to be absolutely sure that you have found the right partner before taking the plunge into marriage.